Walther Ziegler

# Freud
in 60 Minutes

Translated by
Alexander Reynolds

My thanks go to Rudolf Aichner for his tireless critical editing; Silke Ruthenberg for the fine graphics; Lydia Pointvogl, Eva Amberger, Christiane Hüttner, and Dr. Martin Engler for their excellent work as manuscript readers and sub-editors; Prof. Guntram Knapp, who first inspired me with enthusiasm for philosophy; and Angela Schumitz, who handled in the most professional manner, as chief editorial reader, the production of both the German and the English editions of this series of books.

My special thanks go to my translator

Dr Alexander Reynolds.

Himself a philosopher, he not only translated the original German text into English with great care and precision but also, in passages where this was required in order to ensure clear understanding, supplemented this text with certain formulations adapted specifically to the needs of English-language readers.

[…] What decides the purpose of life is simply the programme of the pleasure principle. This principle dominates the operation of the mental apparatus from the start. There can be no doubt about its efficacy, and yet its programme is at loggerheads with the whole world, with the macrocosm as much as with the microcosm.[1]

Bibliographic Information held by the German National Library: The details of the original German edition of this publication are held by the German National Library as part of the German National Bibliography; detailed bibliographical data can be found online at www.dnb.de.

© 2016 Dr Walther Ziegler
1st Edition June 2016
Jacket design and graphic design for the whole book: Silke Ruthenberg, making use of illustrations by:
Raphael Bräsecke, Creative – Studio for Advertising, Comics & Illustrations
© JackF - Fotolia.com (image-frames)
© Valerie Potapova - Fotolia.com (image-frames)
© Svetlana Gryankina - Fotolia.com (speech-balloons)

Publisher and Printing:
BoD – Books on Demand, Norderstedt
ISBN 9783741227707

# Contents

| | |
|---|---|
| **Freud's Great Discovery** | 7 |
| **Freud's Central Idea** | 21 |
|   Oral, Anal and Phallic Stages | 21 |
|   The Oedipus Complex | 27 |
|   The Conflict of the Drives | 31 |
|   The Human Mental Apparatus | 35 |
|   Libido and Drive Satisfaction | 42 |
|   Sublimation | 45 |
|   Repression | 49 |
|   Defence and Symptom-Formation | 51 |
|   Therapy and Transference | 54 |
|   Cure and Psycho-Synthesis | 59 |
|   Id Must Become Ego | 60 |
|   Civilization and its Discontents | 67 |
| **Of What Use is Freud's Discovery for Us Today?** | 71 |
|   Obeying the Pleasure Principle: Maximizing Pleasure and Avoiding Unpleasure | 71 |
|   Id Must Become Ego – From the "Pleasure Principle" to the "Reality Principle" | 72 |

| | |
|---|---|
| Between Scylla and Charybdis – the Secret of Good Upbringing | 75 |
| Anxiety is a Part of Life – Learning to Live Means Learning to Deal with Fear | 78 |
| **Bibliographical References:** | **85** |

# *Freud's Great Discovery*

Sigmund Freud (1856-1939) is without a doubt one of the most important thinkers of the 20th Century. He has marked the way modern Man sees and understands himself more deeply, perhaps, than any other writer. It is largely due to Freud that we nowadays no longer look on ourselves as creatures of pure reason but rather as beings governed by feelings such as anxiety, longing and desire. For two thousand years, philosophy interpreted Man only in terms of his reason. The "I think, therefore I am" of the French philosopher Descartes, for example, amounted to a claim that logical thought formed the essence of what it was to be human. The body was seen as a mere servant of the mind.

Freud fundamentally contradicts this way of seeing things. Man – such was Freud's provocative stance here – is, on the contrary, essentially a creature of drives and instincts, a *homo natura*. It is, first and foremost, these drives, instincts and needs that Man obeys and his mind is just these drives' servant, a mere secondary phenomenon. For, as Freud writes:

> Man is not a being different from animals or superior to them [...].[2]

Our perception of the world and our actions are, said Freud, determined not so much by reason as by feelings and emotions of which we are not aware. We believe, indeed, that we are acting logically and rationally but in fact we are governed by unconscious wishes. If we face the truth, says Freud, we are forced to the conclusion that:

> [...] the human 'I', or 'ego', is not master in its own house.[3]

The philosophers, then, had erred in their overestimation of reason and had, for two thousand years, followed a false path. This radical insight brought down on Freud the hostility of many practicing philosophers. Heidegger accused him of "gawking at states of the soul" and the other great German existentialist Karl Jaspers even dismissed Freud's discovery of unconscious desires and drives as mere "philosophy of the anus". Freud reacted calmly to such criticisms, noting merely that:

> To most people who have been educated in philosophy the idea of anything mental which is not also conscious is so inconceivable that it seems to them absurd and refutable simply by logic.[4]

Philosophers did indeed initially dismiss Freud's idea of an "unconscious mind" as a logical impossibility. If as Freud claimed, they argued, the human psyche comprises an "unconscious realm", then we cannot, by definition, consciously know anything about this realm; it is inaccessible to knowledge and it is impossible that books, such as Freud's, should be written about it. But if, on the other hand, we can in fact seize and know this realm well enough to speak or write about it, then what we seize and know cannot really be called "unconscious"; it must be considered part of our conscious understanding. One way or the other, then, the idea of an "unconscious realm" is superfluous, indeed senseless.

Yet Freud insisted that the unconscious mind did exist, even if it mostly remained inaccessible to rational understanding. He rebutted his critics by specifying that this unconscious mind was something which we do not constantly rationally cognize but rather sporadically recognize. It is in dreams, hypnosis, attacks of laughter or tears, or through involuntary misspeaks, defence mechanisms, symptoms or slips, that what is contained in the unconscious emerges, albeit in disguised form, to the conscious surface of our minds. In dreams, for example, wishes and anxieties that we have pushed out of our waking mind find expression. Some dreams are downright insistent, recurring again and again with slight variations. For Freud, this indicates that unconscious impulses refuse to be simply shut out and repressed. They make sure that they are heard by slipping their message stubbornly into dream after dream. Freud writes:

Only when we pay attention to a dream's specific content, decipher its meaning (which can often be more helpful than we expect), and integrate this meaning into our life, do we free ourselves from these constantly returning impulses out of our unconscious. Dreams, then, can contain helpful messages.

The accounts his patients gave him of their experiences were also, for Freud, evidence of the existence of an unconscious mind. Treating them made him conversant with the phenomenon that people sometimes do things that they do not consciously want to do. Thus patients with a washing compulsion, who wash their hands up to twenty times a day, can find, no matter how hard they think about it, no conscious explanation for this. They are even aware that this constant washing does not improve hygiene but, on the contrary, harms their skin. Not only, then, do they lack a rational explanation for what they do; all their efforts to stop doing it are in vain. From this Freud concludes that there must exist, in addition to consciousness, a second unconscious force which insistently compels to this hand-washing for reasons that remain hidden from the conscious mind.

Another phenomenon which reveals the effects of the unconscious is recurrent bedwetting. First-born children sometimes begin to compulsively wet the bed again, to their own embarrassment, at ages as late as five to ten. This phenomenon mostly occurs when a second child is born and the parents naturally pay more attention to the needier newborn. The firstborn then feels neglected and is jealous of the new arrival – but is also keenly aware that his parents expect him rather to feel glad at having a sibling. The jealousy that he is forced to push out of his consciousness manifests itself through an unconscious, unintentional bedwetting. Sleeping, he slips back into infancy – that is, into a phase of life in which he received all his parents' attention. Freud calls this a "regression", a term derived from the Latin word for "stepping back", i.e. an unconscious retreat into a past state that had been experienced as pleasurable. The interesting thing here is that this behaviour does indeed elicit more attention from the child's parents so that the conflict is solved. This reaction, then, although unconscious, is not without sense and meaning.

Freud's great discovery, then, consists in the insight that the behaviour of the mentally healthy person, no less than that of the mentally ill one, is constantly influenced by unconscious tendencies, conflicts and wishes. Those slips of the tongue and other odd divergences from intended speech or behaviour which have indeed acquired the name "Freudian slips" show the profound force of the unconscious, which plays tricks on reason at every turn. Such "Freudian slips", it has come more and more widely to be acknowledged, often point to a deeper truth.

Although Freud was able to describe this dimension of the unconscious in more and more concrete detail in his many case histories exemplifying regressions, fixations, and other non-rational mechanisms of the human psyche, and was even able effectively to treat neurotic illnesses by psychoanalysis, the reluctance to accept his ideas and therapeutic methods remained very strong. He himself had an interesting explanation for this: his discovery of the unconscious met such a huge degree of resistance because it represented, in his own phrase, a "narcissistic wound", i.e. a painful blow dealt to mankind's collective vanity. Freud saw his own discoveries as the third in a sequence of three great historical "wounds" dealt to Man's vain self-esteem and over-confidence. The first such "wound" – a cosmological one – had been dealt to mankind by Copernicus when he argued that the earth was not the central point of the universe. Since the heavenly bodies do not circle us, we are not the "navel of all Creation" but really only a peripheral cosmic phenomenon. Some centuries later, with Darwin, there was inflicted an analogous "wound" to Man's biological self-image: Man, argued Darwin, is not a being created in God's image but merely a higher mammal. And to Freud himself, finally, there had fallen the sad duty of inflicting, after the cosmological and the biological "wound" to Man's narcissism, yet a third such "wound" in psychological terms. He became bearer of the disturbing message that Man did not, as had been believed for thousands of years, act of his own free rational will but was rather, in large part, the plaything of unconscious drives which remain hidden from Man's own conscious awareness.

Freud's discovery of the unconscious regions of the mind was certainly revolutionary. His researches fundamentally altered our understanding of mental illness. Prior to Freud mental illnesses were treated with such crude methods as ice-cold showers or huge centrifugal mechanisms which turned the patient rapidly in circles so that blood rushed to his head and "the mind could centre itself again". This shows that pre-Freudian psychiatry was largely just groping in the dark in its treatment of mental disorders. Even around 1900, when Freud was publishing his first works, psychiatrists were still warning against train-journeys, believing that the rapidly-changing views from the train window could cause nervous illnesses. In Roman Catholic countries exorcisms were still being practiced in order to drive, through prayer, evil spirits out of the "possessed".

Freud was one of the first to recognize that mental illnesses were not anything that "possessed" people or entered into them from outside but were rather often a consequence of the sufferer's own intimate lived experiences. He noted, among other things, that painful childhood experiences that have not been properly worked through can continue to weigh upon adult life. This new approach called for a whole new science: psychoanalysis. As a trained physician familiar with the natural sciences, Freud had in his earliest researches dissected human nerve fibres in order to find material causes for mental illness; but he soon came to the conclusion that such mental disorders had to, and could be, explained through mental processes alone.

In his medical practice as a doctor specializing in "nervous disorders" he treated patients with the most various symptoms, thus constantly gaining new insights. These insights have been passed on to us through his voluminous published work. He was the founder not only of psychoanalysis – the so-called "talking cure" which treated sufferers from mental disorders not with drugs but through dialogue – but also of an entirely new account of Man and Man's essential nature. Because those "defence mechanisms" and special patterns of behaviour that the mentally ill person uses to handle his daily existence are also used, Freud argued, in barely different forms by the mentally healthy person. Freud was driven by a great passion for revealing these mechanisms common to sick and healthy minds. He saw himself, indeed, as a physician and psychologist but above all as a discoverer, writing that:

# Freud's Great Discovery

> I am actually not at all a man of science, not an observer, not an experimenter, not a thinker. I am by temperament nothing but a conquistador, an adventurer [...] with all the curiosity, daring and tenacity characteristic of a man of this sort.⁶

We might indeed say that Freud, like Columbus, discovered a new continent. He explored a previously unexplored region: that of our wishes, fears and dreams. And just as Columbus, when he set sail with his three ships to prove the earth was round, was declared mad by many of his contemporaries, Freud's theories too met with laughter or hostility, even being dismissed by some as proof of Freud's own personal perversity. Certainly, in prudish turn-of-the-century Austria his discovery of unconscious wishes and of the sexual energies which deeply affect our lives right from birth on represented a massive provocation. Freud's new form of therapy, which involved men and women completely strange to him telling him, on the treatment couch, their most intimate experiences, made Freud a monster in the eyes of many contemporaries. So tremendous was the "new continent" that he had begun to open up.

His work remains controversial even today but one element of his legacy has certainly become accepted wisdom: namely, that one must apply great care in dealing both with one's own psyche and with the psyches of others. No one contests, today, that the human being has certain wishes and drives which he must, in some form or other, live out if he is to remain healthy and deal with everyday life; it is not enough just to work and earn one's living; a person who forbids himself all pleasure and enjoyment and represses the desire to love and be loved will eventually sicken from a sense of a "life unlived". For, as Freud writes:

> All who wish to be more noble-minded than their constitution allows fall victims to neurosis.[7]

We cannot master our own lives if we do not give its due to what Freud calls "the pleasure principle". Every human newborn proceeds according to the formula: "maximize pleasure and minimize unpleasure." The infant follows only the dictates of his basic drives: he suckles when he is hungry, sleeps when he is tired, and cries when he is displeased. Only gradually does there emerge in our lives that second powerful principle which Freud named "the reality principle". As the infant grows into a child there will be demanded of him, at some point, that he acknowledge reality with all its rules and regulations. As the years go by the child is brought to see that he cannot always yield to his drives, that there are rules of hygiene and self-control until finally, in adulthood, pleasure is relegated to a position subordinate to the demands of earning a living. Civilization itself is based upon an agreement to forgo a great deal of what gives us pleasure, a situation addressed in Freud's book *Civilization and Its Discontents*. Freud recognized, indeed, that social rules are important for human coexistence; but when the "discontent" ensuing from having to forgo pleasure becomes too great there is a danger, he argued, of mental illness.

Freud's central idea appears at first to be very simple. Man is a creature of instinct and needs, if he is to live pleasurably and healthily, to fulfil, so far as possible, all his conscious and unconscious wishes. At the same time, he must accept the rules of the society into which he is born. But this raises a whole series of questions.

What limits are to be set to the repression of our drive to pleasure, that is, to the dictates of morality? Indeed, how is morality even possible if Man is, like other animals, a creature of instinct alone? What degree of satisfaction of his or her instinctual drives must a person be allowed in order to remain healthy? Why do we fall ill over a "life unlived"? And what would a truly lived, a genuinely healthy life look like anyway?

# Freud's Central Idea

## Oral, Anal and Phallic Stages

At the start, everything is very simple: the newborn child behaves as pleasure alone dictates; and the source of pleasure is, in the first years of life, the mouth; children of one and two like to suck on their thumbs and indeed on objects in general:

It was the child's first and most vital activity, his sucking at his mother's breast [...] that must have familiarized him with this pleasure. The child's lips, in our view, behave like an erotogenic zone [...]. The satisfaction of the erotogenic zone is associated, in the first instance, with the satisfaction of the need for nourishment.[8]

We designate the very young child as a "breastfeeding baby" because, as Freud points out, sucking at the mother's breast – and the taking of objects into his mouth which he substitutes for this – constitute the first and defining life-experience of such a child. It is through the pleasure felt by his lips and tongue that the very young infant first perceives the world. Freud calls this first development of the pleasure principle the "oral stage". Other sources of pleasure are added, of course, as time moves on; but, as can be proven from observation in all the cultures of the world, the original form of human pleasure is that which the child derives from touching and experiencing the world around him with his mouth. That breastfeeding is for the child an experience of intense pleasure is, in Freud's view, an unquestionable fact and can be plainly observed:

No one who has seen a baby sinking back satiated from the breast and falling asleep with flushed cheeks and a blissful smile can escape the reflection that this picture persists as a prototype of the expression of sexual satisfaction in later life.[9]

Even more plainly in the case of a baby's dummy, which does not nourish but clearly gives pleasure. It is, so to speak, the first of many pleasures that will come to substitute the initial pleasure of the mother's breast.

During the second or third year of life there is added to the oral source of pleasure a second such source. The child, when defecating, gradually realizes, to his own astonishment, that he is capable of producing something. He can retain his faeces or release it. In learning to master his organs of defecation he acquires a sense of being able to affect his environment without the help of those parents whom he has hitherto perceived as all-powerful. Freud calls this the "anal stage". That the small child assigns such great significance to merely going to the toilet may, at first, seem laughable. For adults this "activity" barely counts as one at all, since the forms of "production" that grownups and even older children draw their self-esteem from – the schoolboy from his schoolwork, the carpenter from his table, the mechanic from his repaired car, or even the housewife from her daily cooking and washing – are activities of a quite different order. But a two-year-old child, as Freud points out, has hitherto had no chance to produce any effect on the world at all. No wonder, then, that it is an epoch-making event for him to find that he can produce something. Something, moreover, that stinks and often provokes a great reaction from the adults around him, especially if it has been "produced" at a place not set aside for it. Such an event is the signal for training in hygiene to begin. Children are henceforth trained to "go" only "on the potty" and their "production", they are told, is something dirty and disgusting. Thus, a first "taboo" is built up. The child's perception of the world – initially unrestrictedly pleasurable – is confronted for the first time with the rules and prohibitions of adult society. Controlling its own faeces is thus the first step in "acculturation" that the little human being is forced to take. If this inculcation of taboos and training in hygiene is carried out too early and too fast, it can lead even at this early stage to the child's developing severe frustrations, which can sometimes have effects reaching into adult life.

Thus Freud speaks of having discovered, in patients displaying certain compulsive behavioural symptoms, an "anal-sadistic" character distinguished by pedantry and authoritarianism. If a child, for example, is compelled too soon, by the threat of having his parents' love withdrawn from him or by actual physical force, to "go on the potty", this child can develop an attitude of spiteful, stubborn "retentiveness" vis-à-vis the grownup world, which manifests itself again, once he himself has grown up, in the form of a fixed "character type": that of the miser or the "control freak". Freud calls the "anal stage" also the "anal-sadistic stage" because there develops, side by side with the child's increasing control of his bowel functions, also a first inclination toward aggression. Children now begin to pull wings off flies, adopt an aggressively investigative attitude to the world, and even start, as soon as they have begun to master language, to speak rudely to their mothers. Freud notes that a child often draws such rude speech specifically from the taboo sphere of "anality". He sees the presence in almost all cultures of insults related to the "ass" and "asshole" as a telling indication of the great importance of this early placing of all that is "anal" under a taboo.

In the third (or at the latest fourth or fifth) year of life yet another source of pleasure, after the mouth and the anus, begins to play a central role in the child's experience: namely, the genitals. There now gradually develops a pleasure focussed on the penis or the clitoris. Children begin to play with their own, or other children's, sexual organs. It is the period of "doctors and nurses" games, when children first become aware of essential differences between boys and girls and seek out their first "love interests":

> The sexual instinct has hitherto been predominantly auto-erotic; it now finds a sexual object.[10]

Whereas previously what Freud calls "libido" had been invested only in the child's own body or in such objects as teddy bears, this libido is now directed toward real "significant others". First and foremost, says Freud, toward the mother, since she tends always to be closest at hand. Freud insists that there is nothing abnormal or pathological about a small boy of four or five being actually erotically in love with his mother. This enamourment, moreover, is largely an unconscious matter. Freud speaks here of the "Oedipus complex".

## Freud's Central Idea

## *The Oedipus Complex*

In the ancient Greek tragedy that bears his name Oedipus was a king of Thebes who is cast out of his native city as a child but returns there, unaware of his own history, as a young man. In his ignorance of who he is, he kills a man encountered on his way, who is in fact his father, and eventually marries this man's wife: his own mother. Finally discovering the truth about what he has done, shame prompts him to put out his own eyes. This ancient drama, claims Freud, is repeated over and over, albeit in less bloody and grotesque a form, in family homes all over the world:

> While he is still a small child, a son will already begin to develop a special affection for his mother, whom he regards as belonging to him; he begins to feel his father as a rival who disputes his sole possession.[11]

Boys aged four to six generally choose their own mother as their first erotically-charged "love object" but are aware, even as they do so, that this choice is a forbidden one. They sense already that it is really only the father who can share this sort of relationship with the mother. The father himself makes this clear. Since a five- or six-year-old boy will already often have observed that little girls have no penis, he will easily (even if unconsciously) develop the idea that, if he acts upon his desire for his mother, his father will punish him by taking away his penis. The father, of course, never explicitly threatens castration but the idea is there in the male child's mind.

Freud himself recognizes that the father's role as upholder of the taboo on incest is an important one, inasmuch as the son is thereby forced to choose another, more viable love-object than his own mother. But an unconscious anger toward the father persists nonetheless and the son plays with the thought of killing the father. At the same time, though, he has a bad conscience about this anger since he ought not, nor does he want, to hate his own father. Besides the incest taboo there are now built up by the mother and father, around this initial bad conscience, many other moral rules and prohibitions. Thus, the "Oedipus complex" forms the core of our conscience or, as Freud calls it, our "super-ego".

The super-ego develops in a similar manner in girls.

They too have a sort of "Oedipus complex", although they do not, of course, fear castration. Girls too first choose their mother as their original love-object but turn, around age four at the latest, toward their father, once they have realized that they are of the same sex as the mother. Here it is the mother who plays the role of constraining force. She compels the daughter to keep at a distance from the father, thus internalizing the incest taboo. The "Oedipus complex", then, is, in Freud's view, a completely normal stage of maturation in the psycho-sexual development of both boys and girls and thus a component part of every parent-child relationship:

> I do not wish to assert that the Oedipus complex exhausts the relation of children to their parents. It can easily be far more complex. The Oedipus complex can, moreover, be developed to a greater or lesser strength [...]. But it is a regular and very important factor in a child's mental life.[12]

The taboo placed on erotic love for mother or father takes hold deep in the unconscious and forms the core of the super-ego. In this way children learn to comply with basic rules of morality. Thus, whereas the suckling infant had lived according to the "pleasure principle" alone, there is added, in the anal and phallic stages, a second principle: the "reality principle". Children must now deal with reality. They control their own defecation, learn to respect the toys of other children, and comply with the incest taboo. But in other areas children have, as yet, no inner censor and continue to follow the "pleasure principle": by loudly expressing their wishes they usually achieve, indeed, the aim their instincts push them to pursue, be it a bag of sweets or a ride on the carousel.

Two factors are decisive at this early stage. Firstly, children experience, from the very beginning, pleasure in its oral, anal and (later) genital forms. In puberty, these so-called "partial drives" unite, but under the dominance of genital sexuality. Secondly, Freud recognized that human personality development begins already with these early experiences of pleasure. This is true not only as regards the fixing of "character types" but also as regards specific sexual preferences. Thus, Freud discovered, in the course of treating his patients, that penchants for high heels, nylon stockings and other fetishes were mostly to be traced back to fixations of the libido in early childhood. Man, then, is a being influenced by sexual pleasure not just in adulthood but from the moment of birth on.

## The Conflict of the Drives

Freud, however, studied not just the development of the sexual drive but also the emergence of conscience. He could observe in his own patients what an enormous pressure conscience can exert on an individual. He also asked himself the question: just how does the pleasure- and instinct-driven child become, in the end, a moral, law-abiding adult who complies with rules and conventions? He himself could not, initially, understand how neurotic illness was even possible. If Man was, as Freud assumed, a creature entirely dominated by instincts that lived by the "pleasure principle" and always obeyed his strongest need of the moment, the question naturally arose of why repression of desires, and thereby neurotic symptoms, should ever occur at all. To answer this question was all the harder for him because he aspired to explain all phenomena scientifically and could not, for example, admit the idea of conscience as some divinely-inspired power. For Freud, the entire mental realm did indeed have to be explained in terms of the drives we share with other animals. Nevertheless, he saw many patients who clearly suffered from "pangs of conscience". In many cases the moral demands that these patients placed on themselves were even harsher than those society placed on them:

> In such people we regularly find indications of a contention between wishful impulses or, as we are in the habit of saying, a psychical conflict. One part of the personality champions certain wishes while another part opposes them and fends them off. Without such a conflict there is no neurosis.[13]

That repression, by the individual, of his own wishes – i.e. his refusal to satisfy his own drives – which is the work of human conscience leads, then, to a conflict in which self-formed wishes clash with self-imposed prohibitions. But what was the origin of this bad conscience, this feeling of having failed and not lived up to one's own standards, which caused such difficulties to so many of Freud's patients? Freud's answer here is simple. From infancy on, the individual takes up taboos and prohibitions into his own mind. He internalizes them and identifies with them. That is to say, the child takes everything that parents, teachers, the church, books and other moral authorities say to him and stores it in his conscience, the so-called "super-ego". And an individual's super-ego has the capacity to turn against what gives this same individual pleasure. In this respect, Freud, concedes, Man is distinct from other animals after all. Man alone can come into conflict with his own intentions and even develop, as a result, neurotic illnesses:

A dissension of this kind may perhaps only occur in human beings and, on that account, neurosis may, generally speaking, constitute their prerogative over the animals.[14]

An animal, says Freud, cannot develop neuroses since it knows no moral scruples but, sure in its instincts, simply follows the healthiest path. It always yields to whatever impulse is strongest in it. A dog that desires to eat a bone but at the same time fears a larger dog that it sees approaching may either fight or run away – but it will not torture itself with this dilemma for weeks. But a human being who is stressed and overtaxed by his job and his boss will, even though his instincts tell him to quit, put up with this situation for months or years for purely rational reasons – e.g. because the job is financially advantageous – until he eventually, perhaps, becomes neurotically ill. Neurotic symptoms can, indeed, be artificially produced even in animals if they are placed under high stress in laboratories; in the wild, however, any animal would simply withdraw from such stress. Man, by contrast, regularly makes greater demands on himself than he can handle. The human mind possesses a capacity that is both astonishing and perilous: that of avoiding internal conflicts, denying and repressing them and leaving them unresolved until they actually make the mind sick. For Freud, then, mental illness is nothing other than a particular way of dealing with drives and the conflict between drives. Indeed, where such conflicts arise neurotic and even psychotic ways of behaving can occur even in the lives of otherwise healthy people. Freud describes this with the aid of his model of the human mental apparatus.

## The Human Mental Apparatus

Freud believed that the apparatus of the human mind consisted of three parts. He did not, of course, mean this in a physical sense corresponding to parts of the brain. The term that Freud used for these "parts" was actually "Instanz", meaning "instance" in the sense of a "court of the first instance", "court of the second instance" and so on. In other words, Freud's idea was of a functional rather than a physical division of the human mind, with each specific mental structure having specific "authority" over certain types of mental content. The three "instances" are called the id, the ego, and the super-ego. The id is the region of drives, wishes, fears, desires and pleasures. Freud describes it as:

> [...] a chaos, a cauldron full of seething excitations [...]. It is filled with energy reaching it from the instincts, but it has no organization [...].[15]

The id obeys no rational rules. It embodies pleasure and the "pleasure principle". The lives of newborns and small children are entirely lives of the id. It is the original, and remains the largest, region of human mental activity.

The second mental "instance" is the super-ego, commonly called the "conscience". There gather and settle in the super-ego moral concepts and religious and social taboos and prohibitions which the individual has internalized, from childhood on, out of the teachings of parents, school and society. The super-ego contains, for example, such moral commandments as "thou shalt not kill", "thou shalt honour thy father and thy mother" and "thou shalt not steal".

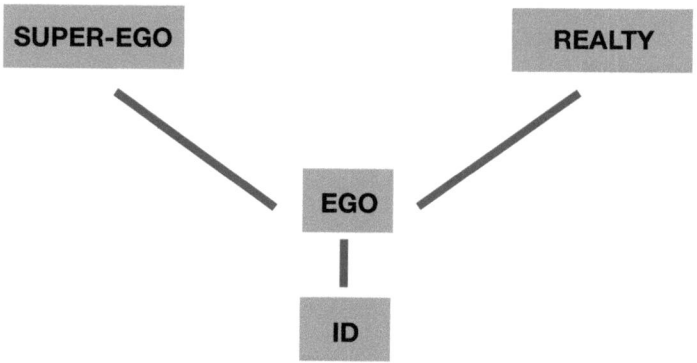

The third "instance", the so-called "ego", is, so to speak, the "switchboard" from which everything must be coordinated. The ego has the difficult task of satisfying the instinct-driven desires emerging from

## Freud's Central Idea

the id while at the same time granting their due to the restrictions and admonitions of the super-ego. The ego tests the state of reality and must subordinate desires, drives and the actions that ensue from them to the "reality principle". The id, on the other hand, obeys only the "pleasure principle". Freud describes the difficult task of the ego in the following terms:

> We are warned by a proverb against serving two masters at the same time. The poor ego has things even worse: it serves three severe masters and does what it can to bring their claims and demands into harmony with one another. These claims are always divergent and often seem incompatible. No wonder that the ego so often fails in its task. Its three tyrannical masters are the external world, the super-ego and the id.[16]

Freud emphasizes that this model of the human mind is not intended as a contribution to mental pathology but rather as one to "anthropology" – and to "anthropology", moreover, in the literal and original ancient Greek sense of "an account of the nature of Man". In other words, Freud's intention here was not just to explain mental illness but rather the function of the human mind in general. Freud made, one might say, no essential distinction between normal and pathological ways of behaving. The basic patterns, he claimed, are the same and the line between 'normal' and 'neurotic' is a blurred and shifting one. At every moment of our lives the three "instances" id, ego and super-ego are working feverishly together, struggling to establish what is the right thing to do in the face of reality.

Imagine, for example, a young man walking along the street who sees some newspapers piled in a case which also has a slot for the coin each paper costs. On their front page is the image of a beautiful woman and the headline: "Scandal! Secret Naked Photos of Pamela Anderson!" Immediately the voice of the id is heard: "Take the newspaper out of the case!"

But in the same moment the young man's ego recognizes that he has left his wallet at home and has no money on him. The id, however, insists and, obeying the "pleasure principle", urges: "Don't worry about that. No one is looking. Just take the newspaper!"

## Freud's Central Idea

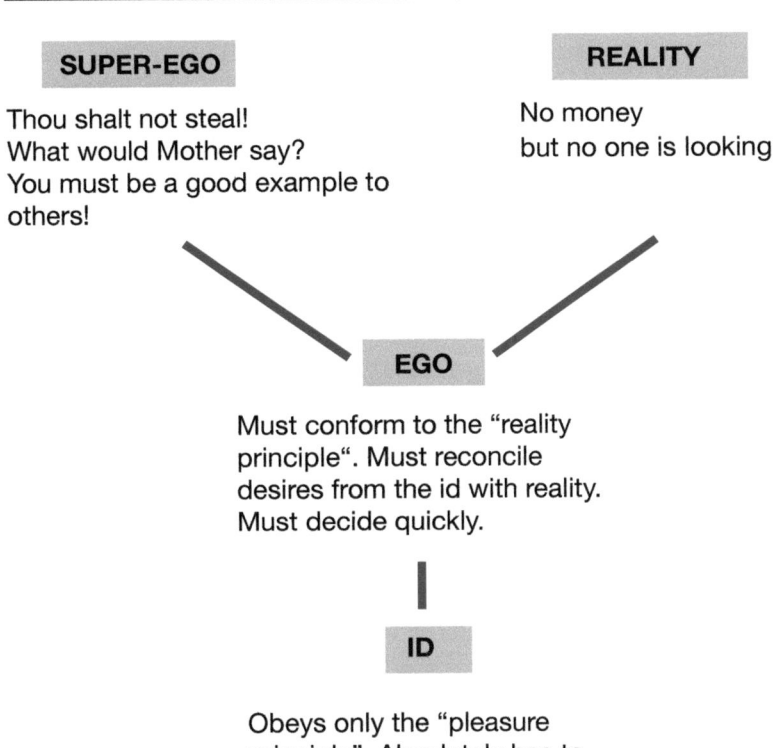

The ego now does indeed test reality to judge whether it might be feasible to take the newspaper without paying. But here the voice of the super-ego is heard, asking: "Are you mad? That would be stealing! Stealing is out of the question. Even if you are not caught it is not fair to cheat the newspaper-seller out of his earnings. You need always to behave in a way that is an example for others. What would happen if everyone took newspapers without paying? And what would Mother say?" All this happens in just a split second. If the ego yields to the initial impulse from the id, this will call forth impulses toward self-punishment from the super-ego; but if the poor ego decides rather to repress the id's desire, this in turn will result in massive feelings of displeasure. The ego, then, is in a quandary. It has a conflict. Freud writes:

> Thus the ego, driven by the id, confined by the super-ego, repulsed by reality, struggles to master its 'economic' task [...] and we can understand how it is that so often we cannot suppress a cry: 'Life is not easy!'[17]

We see here how deeply sceptical Freud was about that "freedom of the human will" that most philosophers have thought so highly of. We see, in fact, little of the much-praised "freedom of consciousness" – which for Sartre, for example, was Man's essential distinguishing feature – in this ego beset on all sides.

## Freud's Central Idea

Freud rather compares Man's "free will" with a rather helpless horseman who attempts, indeed, to control his horse – i.e. the animalistic drives emerging from the id – and to guide it in the right direction but who is not, in fact, able to master his powerful steed:

(Just as) a rider, if he is not to be parted from his horse, is obliged to guide it where it wants to go, so in the same way the ego is in the habit of transforming the id's will into action as if it were its own.[18]

Freud has a specific name for this capacity of the human ego to first yield to instinct and then afterward to seek out a non-instinctual, rational explanation for what one has done: "rationalization". Although reason believes that it has determined the action taken, in fact reason only justifies, after the fact, a decision already dictated by irrational drives. Freud's model of the drives and their conflict becomes still clearer when we consider the different ways we have of dealing with the energy of which these drives consist.

## Libido and Drive Satisfaction

What drives Man on in his life is always one fundamental energy which Freud calls "libido":

> Libido is an expression taken from the theory of the emotions. We call by that name the energy, regarded as a quantitative magnitude (though not at present actually measurable), of all those instincts which have to do with all that may be comprised under the word 'love'.[19]

The id, as the realm of drives and desires, is described by Freud not only as a chaos and a seething cauldron of stimuli but, in one passage, as a "reservoir of libido". By "libido" here Freud means the totality of drive-energy within the id. Freud holds, indeed, the sexual drive to be the strongest of all drives motivating human beings but sexual energy is itself just a

## Freud's Central Idea

part of this libido. There belong likewise to this libido the energy that a mother directs toward her child, or a child towards its siblings, its friends or its teddy-bear. Freud defines "libido" as follows:

> [...] we do not separate from this – what, in any case, has a share in the name 'love' – on the one hand self-love and, on the other, love for parents and children, friendship and love for humanity in general, and also devotion to concrete objects and to abstract ideas.[20]

Libido, as the core energy of Man, cannot, indeed, presently be measured; but it is nonetheless a quantitative magnitude with which the ego has somehow to deal. According to Freud there are four possible ways of dealing with it: direct drive-satisfaction; sublimation; repression; or defence in the form of symptom-formation. The following diagram shows, once again, the three "instances" forming the human mental apparatus: id, ego and super-ego, but this time with the addition of the aspect that Freud calls "the economy of the drives":

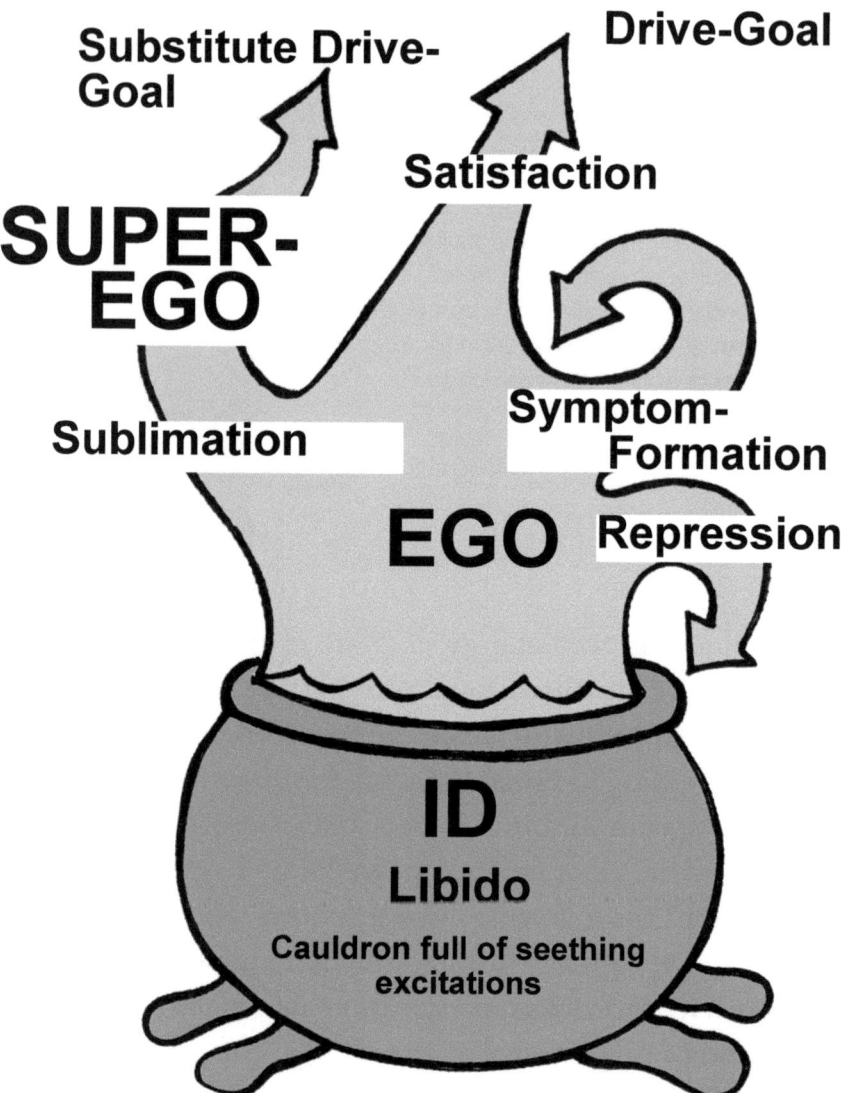

## Freud's Central Idea

The simplest of all the various possible scenarios over which the ego must preside is that whereby the drives of the id are directly satisfied: after a brief testing of external reality, the ego guides the libido directly to its desired drive-goal and the drive is satisfied without a problem. For example, a young man sitting in a café on a spring day sees a charming young woman at the next table. He smiles and she smiles back. The id immediately makes its wishes known. The ego reacts, plucks up courage and begins to flirt with the young woman. A wonderful romance develops and that very night all the young man's libidinous wishes are fulfilled. The drive-goal is attained.

## *Sublimation*

We know, however, that not all such wishes can be fulfilled so quickly and easily. There is, says Freud, a second possibility: namely, to "sublimate" libido, i.e. to redirect the drive toward some other goal than its original one. Let us assume that, in the case just described, the ego hesitates for several minutes to speak to the young woman, fearing rejection, even despite the constant urging of the id to "Do something! This is the girl of your dreams!", until finally it is too late: the young woman is joined at her table by another young man who kisses her and is evidently her boyfriend or husband. In such a situation the disappointed ego may well redirect the dammed-up libidinous energy toward some more easily attainable goal and instead, for example, order a beer or a cream tart – a poor substitute, indeed, but a gain in pleasure nonetheless. There arise in daily life many such situations in which, instead of our original drive-goal, we must make do with some sort of substitute satisfaction:

> This capacity to exchange its originally sexual aim for another one, which is no longer sexual but which is psychically related to the first aim, is called the capacity for sublimation.[21]

Classic examples of such sublimation were to be observed in those pre-"co-educational" secondary schools which existed in many European countries right up until the 1970s. One of the rationales for separating boys and girls in this way was that the libidinous energies that pupils of each sex would tend naturally to direct toward co-pupils of the opposite sex would thus have to be re-channeled into the material being taught them – i.e. the sex-drive would be sublimated into improved educational performance:

(The sexual instinct) places extraordinarily large amounts of force at the disposal of civilized activity, and it does this in virtue of its especially marked characteristic of being able to displace its aim without materially diminishing its intensity.[22]

Scholars and scientists also practice sublimation when they devote whole days and nights to their research. Freud, indeed, thought that all the cultural achievements of any society – its art, music, religion, philosophy and law – are founded ultimately in the sublimation of basic animal drives. Culture obliges people to place a part of their personal energy at its disposal by establishing laws and moral taboos which prevent, or at least restrict, people's direct living-out of their drives and instincts.

Another simple but topical example of the targeted sublimation and redirection of libidinal energy is to be found in the world of sport. It is well known that no women are allowed into the training camps for World Cup footballers. This is especially strictly forbidden on the night before an important match. There have been many scandals involving players particularly susceptible to the call of their "drives" disregarding this taboo and slipping out over the camp fence.

The point of this forced asceticism is, of course, to induce in the young players what Freud would call a "damming up" of the sex-drive, whereby this "dammed-up" libido merges, furthermore, with aggressive drives emanating from the id. The result of this is that, once the players are on the pitch, they unconsciously transfer this aggression and anger onto those whom they can imagine to be the cause of their enforced drive-repression, the opposing team, and thereby play with greater commitment and "fighting spirit".

If, by contrast, the young sportsmen were allowed to spend the night before the game with their wives or girlfriends, they would go onto the pitch relaxed and satisfied – and consequently lose. This strategic application, in professional sport, of the sublimation of libidinal drive-energy into aggressive resolution may seem a trivial matter; but anthropologists have confirmed that Indian tribesmen too often lived ascetic lives prior to going to war and substituted ritual war-dances for sexual intercourse in order to work themselves into the right mood of aggression. The process, then, that Freud calls sublimation – i.e. the redirection of drive-energy toward a different goal than its initial one – is an ancient and widespread capacity of human beings, and one to which we largely owe the establishment of human culture.

## *Repression*

The third possible way in which libido can be dealt with is repression. This means that the ego sees itself as able neither to facilitate the drive's attainment of its initial goal nor to engage in sublimation. It pushes, therefore, the wishes and desires in question completely out of mind, i.e. "represses" them. Repression occurs constantly every day. When the alarm clock rings in the morning, most people feel a strong desire from their id to go on sleeping. But the ego must check reality, look at the alarm clock, and admit to itself that it is indeed time to get up and go to work. The ego represses, having no choice, the desire emerging from the id.

But the unconscious mind sometimes uses very imaginative strategies in order to get, after all, its wish to carry on sleeping. It can exploit the fact that the ego is, in this situation, not yet fully awake and functioning. Many people tell, for example, of how they heard the alarm clock in the morning but went on sleeping because the sound was taken up and absorbed into a dream – becoming, for example, the sound of a train rushing by in some dream about a rail journey. During sleep the id alone has sway and translates its repressed desires and conflicts into dream-images; in the early morning when the conscious mind has not yet taken back control it can easily be "cheated" by the id and held in sleep. But in most cases the ego wins out and the id's desire to go on sleeping is repressed. The dangerous thing about repression is the fact that, although the repressed libido may be banished from the conscious ego, it does not thereby just disappear; it remains present in the unconscious. And this means that the pressure for a "return of the repressed" becomes ever greater – especially when the repressed desires are not just trivial wishes but needs fundamental to the life of an individual.

## *Defence and Symptom-Formation*

In the case where too great a proportion of an individual's vitally necessary needs and desires are not allowed to be fulfilled – be this for moral reasons or out of regard for others – then this individual's repressed libido will tend to turn permanently against his or her own ego. Or, as Freud puts it:

All who wish to be more noble-minded than their constitution allows fall victims to neurosis.[23]

An individual can then fall ill from a sense of "life unlived". He has more and more difficulty restraining his id and finally begins to display compulsive behaviour or symptoms of neurosis – such as depression, migraine, hysterical attacks, compulsive washing, twitches or paralyses – or even psychosis – such as hearing voices, megalomania, or a persecution complex. Repressed vital wishes can also result in physical illnesses. Generally, every mental illness can be understood as the consequence of a situation of stress in which the ego finds itself no longer able to fulfil its task. It succumbs to anxiety either vis-à-vis its own drives or vis-à-vis reality. Depending on which anxiety is primary the ego flees either into neurosis or into psychosis. But both are defence mechanisms for an ego that feels strained beyond its powers. Freud gives a very clear and acute definition of these two main groups of mental illness: the neuroses and the psychoses:

> Neurosis does not disavow the reality, it only ignores it; psychosis disavows it and tries to replace it.[24]

Neurosis functions as a defence mechanism and a refuge for the ego inasmuch as the person falling mentally ill usually becomes, due to the complaints thus arising, unfit for work and less is expected of him generally. This means the neurotic can flee reality without denying it.

The psychotic, on the other hand, takes issue precisely with reality. Not, indeed, by changing it or by fleeing it but simply by inventing a second world for himself which he finds more acceptable. The classic image of the patient who has constructed his own personal perception of reality is the man who thinks he is Napoleon and holds insistently to this role in all his dealings with the world.

In literature, Don Quixote is the incarnation of such a psychotic personality. He insists – in the face of all contrary reality – on believing, and making others believe, he is a knight living a medieval world of noble lords and ladies.

The mentally healthy individual, then, defined against this background, would be the one who neither flees from reality and its stressful demands nor creates a fantasy world in place of this latter, but rather works resolutely to really change the world that confronts him:

> [...] This expedient, normal behaviour leads to work being carried out on the external world; it does not stop, as in psychosis, at effecting internal changes. It is no longer autoplastic but alloplastic.[25]

## *Therapy and Transference*

If mental illness, then, is a consequence of the ego's collapsing under the strains of reality, the ungovernable desires of the id, or the self-imposed strictures of the super-ego, the goal of psychotherapy must consist in fortifying the weakened ego until it can once again take on the tasks it needs to perform:

> The ego is weakened by the internal conflict and we must go to its help [...]. We assure the patient of the strictest discretion and place at his service our experience at interpreting material that has been influenced by the unconscious. Our knowledge is to [...] give his ego back its mastery over lost provinces of his mental life.[26]

This rehabilitation of the ego is achieved by drawing back into consciousness those conflicts, often repressed ones, which lie at the root of the patient's mental disturbance. The conflicts themselves cannot, of course, so long after their initial emergence, be solved by the course of therapy. Freud himself was clearly aware of this, writing that:

> When I have promised my patients help or improvement by means of a cathartic treatment I have often been faced by this objection: 'Why, you tell me yourself that my illness is probably connected with my circumstances and the events of my life. You cannot alter these in any way. How do you propose to help me, then?' And I have been able to make this reply: 'No doubt fate would find it easier than I do to relieve you of your illness. But you will be able to convince yourself that much will be gained if we succeed in transforming your hysterical misery into common unhappiness. With a mental life that has been restored to health you will be better armed against that unhappiness.[27]

The point of psychoanalytic therapy, then, is not to try to alter the past but only to alter the way in which past events are remembered and experienced. The "transforming of hysterical misery into common unhappiness" is achieved here by making unconscious traumatizations finally conscious. But this must not be misunderstood as a process of gaining knowledge through the simple application of reason. The patient is not questioned or advised by the psychoanalyst; nor does the analyst try to convince him of anything by argument. Rather it is through the non-rational process of "free association" that the patient can rediscover these buried conflicts, sometimes even living through them again on the emotional plane. The psychoanalyst helps the patient here, of course – but again, not with clever advice or words of encouragement but on the contrary by withdrawing and making himself "transparent". The analyst sits with his back to the patient, or off to the side, leaving this latter entirely to his own feelings and memories. So as to be able to remember all the more freely the patient himself does not sit but lies on a couch.

The psychoanalyst is further aided in his work by a phenomenon which we also observe in everyday life: so-called "transference". The psychoanalyst, says Freud, can only benefit the patient if he makes himself available to him as a kind of mirror, a surface of projection. The patient can then "transfer" to the analyst his feelings about whatever person in his past may have given rise to the inner conflict he suffers from and in this way live this conflict through again within the analysis. The analyst may thus take on, for the patient, the role of the father, the mother, or some other person with whom the patient has had, in the distant past, a problematical relationship. This can lead to reproaches, pleas for forgiveness or even vituperation as well as other outbursts of emotion, being directed by the patient at the analyst. But the analyst must accept these without reaction or even comment, so as to allow free rein to the healthy cathartic effect of the revivification of the buried conflict. The core, then, of the psychoanalytic cure is not the rational intellectual understanding of those things or events, past or present, that may be causing the patient's illness but rather the reviving, on the emotional plane, of past conflicts. It is not a matter of bringing repressed feeling back into consciousness and rationally understanding them but rather of living them through once again and learning how to handle them differently.

## *Cure and Psycho-Synthesis*

This, says Freud, brings about a shift in the emotional weight ascribed to encounters, memories and situations which benefits the patient's wellbeing. Thus, a situation which one might hitherto have experienced as unbearably humiliating is, after therapy, seen as just an everyday case of embarrassment. Freud emphasizes here that this emotional reevaluation of the past is one which is carried out spontaneously by the patient, not artificially imposed by the psychoanalyst:

The psycho-synthesis is thus achieved during analytical treatment without our intervention, automatically and inevitably. We have created the conditions for it by breaking up the symptoms into their elements and by removing the resistances. It is not true that something in the patient has been divided and is now quietly waiting for us to somehow put it together again.[28]

Psychoanalysis aims, then, ultimately at drawing unconscious fixations, compulsions, and other inhibitions out into the light of waking consciousness, so as to shatter the subliminal power through which they hinder the patient's enjoyment of a full life. The task is to take repressed drives, unmastered disappointments and traumatic past experiences and to make of them simple recollections which, even if they have not been thoroughly worked through and dealt with, are henceforth at least accessible to consciousness.

## *Id Must Become Ego*

This apparently simple sentence has, in fact, three meanings in Freud's work. Firstly, ideas repressed back into the id must, through therapy, be once again made accessible to the conscious ego. Secondly, the remark applies also to the development of the child into an adult: the child, which initially obeys only the chaotic and spontaneous "pleasure principle" – i.e. that of the id – must learn, as it progresses toward adulthood, to take the "reality principle" too into account. That is to say, the child must form for itself an ego that can control its basic needs and guide them toward reasonable ends:

> Where id was, there ego shall be.[29]

But this demand applies not just to the individual but to society as a whole. And herein lies the third meaning of the short phrase. Freud considers religion too to be a collective illusion which is nourished by the wishes and fears of the id. The life-drive and the libidinal desire for unlimited enjoyment of pleasure that arise out of the id cannot be satisfied by the ego because reality always holds such disappointments as sickness and privation in store. But above all the "pleasure principle" collides in a fundamental way with the simple fact that we are mortal. The ego has no recipe against death. In order, then, not to be confronted constantly with this fact of mortality the ego flees into religious faith – in Freud's eyes a kind of collective psychosis. The ego "hallucinates", as it were, an eternal life after death. To the intense desire for immortality there corresponds, says Freud, an equally intense belief in an other-worldly Paradise:

> These (religious ideas) which are given out as teachings are not precipitates of experience or end-results of thinking: they are illusions, fulfilments of the oldest, strongest and most urgent wishes of mankind. The secret of their strength lies in the strength of those wishes.[30]

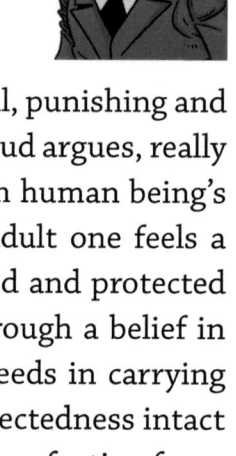

God – conceived of as an all-powerful, punishing and comforting Heavenly Father – is, Freud argues, really nothing else but a projection of each human being's real, corporeal father. Even as an adult one feels a need for the sense of being sheltered and protected that one felt in early childhood. Through a belief in "the Heavenly Father" the ego succeeds in carrying over the infantile experience of protectedness intact into adult life. But the price for the comforting function is a kind of psychotic flight from reality. Religious ceremonial too, with its strikingly repetitive quality, has something of the character of a compulsion and tends to prevent Man's becoming conscious.

The Christian practice of the eating of the so-called

"host", which the church calls "the body of Christ", is, argues Freud, an ancient ritual intended to strengthen the psyche by identification with the powerful Heavenly Father. This sort of behaviour – i.e. the ritual assumption of identity with a being by eating of him – is also to be found in many primitive societies. Often, a totemic animal is consumed in a collective meal so that its aura and strength pass over into all the participants.

But, says Freud, however effectively this belief in a life after death in Paradise may distract us from the real fragility of our existence, it too must yield to the watchword: 'Id must become ego!' Mankind must leave its childhood behind and cast off the illusion that there is a protecting God in heaven:

(Human beings) will, it is true, find themselves in a difficult situation. They will have to admit to themselves the full extent of their helplessness

> and their insignificance in the machinery of the universe; they can no longer be the centre of creation, no longer the object of tender care on the part of a beneficient Providence. They will be in the same position as a child who has left the parental house where he was so warm and comfortable. But surely infantilism is destined to be surmounted [...].[31]

Freud considers philosophy too to be, much like religion, a grand illusion. He even draws an analogy between philosophy and hallucinatory mental illness:

> [...] And the delusions of paranoiacs have an unpalatable external similarity and internal kinship to the systems of our philosophers.[32]

Philosophers attempt, as do many paranoiacs, to interpret the whole world, and to order and control it, in terms of what is really just one of its aspects. For Nietzsche this was "will to power"; for Hegel the "World Spirit"; for Kant the faculty of reason; for Marx the relations of production. Each of these philosophers traced, in a "compulsive" manner, all phenomena back to their respective key idea.

This key "world-ordering" idea can be, in the case of certain paranoiacs, something as trivial as hair-colour. They might feel persecuted or systematically cheated by people with blond hair. They might interpret the whole of society, indeed the world, in light of the idea that blond people have more power, opportunities and advantages than those with brown hair and put the blame for all their failures on their belonging to the latter group. They discover this disadvantagement in everday life again and again, since this is the only angle they want to look at the world from. They note that newscasters are always blond, as are film stars. But the legal system too is dominated by fair-haired people, so that blondes are always sentenced less harshly. "Dumb blonde" jokes may be an exception to this rule; but their denigration of blondes is only a way of dealing with the deeply-felt inferiority of brown-haired people.

Freud considers the attempts by the great philosophers to reduce, with their systems, the diversity of the world to the one idea that obsesses them to be symptomatic of a similar compulsive disorder. In this way they repress the fact that the phenomena of reality as we encounter it cannot be controlled. Just like religion, philosophy promises Man an explanation of the world which is in principle impossible.

For Freud, however, philosophy is nowhere near as dangerous as religion, since the complicated systems of the philosophers will always be read only by very few people. Religion, on the other hand, has a vast influence and prevents, with its great empty promises, Man from devoting himself to his true calling. Man, says Freud, should take the energy he devotes to the "beyond" and invest it in the "here-below":

> By withdrawing their expectations from the 'other world' and concentrating all their liberated energies into their life on earth, they will probably succeed in achieving a state of things in which life will become tolerable for everyone and civilization no longer oppressive to anyone.[33]

We can gather already from these words that Freud is concerned that many people may feel "stifled" by civilized life. He has a rather sceptical view of society with its religious and moral rules.

## *Civilization and its Discontents*

Freud consistently critiqued traditional norms and called for a freer development of human beings in which more room was made for desire and pleasure. It is no wonder, he believed, that so many people become ill, depressive or neurotic, since society hardly gives them the chance to develop themselves and to live pleasurable lives:

If, however, a culture has not got beyond a point at which the satisfaction of one portion of its participants depends upon the suppression of another, and perhaps larger, portion – and this

> is the case in all present-day cultures – it is understandable that the suppressed people should develop an intense hostility toward (the culture in question).³⁴

> It goes without saying that a culture which leaves so large a number of its participants unsatisfied and drives them into revolt neither has, nor deserves, the prospect of a lasting existence.³⁵

It is no wonder, then, that in Freud's late work, *Civilization and Its Discontents,* he places great emphasis on the latter of these two terms: the discomfort felt by many under the pressure of civilized forms of life. But on the other hand Freud fully recognized that a

## Freud's Central Idea

society with rules and laws is an absolute necessity, since the human being is characterized by a dangerous potential for aggression:

> The existence of this inclination to aggression, which we can detect in ourselves and justly assume to be present in others, is the factor which disturbs our relations with our neighbour and which forces civilization into such a high expenditure of energy.[36]

The coexistence of human beings in society can only succeed if civilization proves able to anchor in its members' individual super-egos moral values providing a sense of right and wrong. Indeed, moral commandments and prohibitions have been used since time immemorial to keep the naked "pleasure principle" – i.e. the ruthlessly egotistical pursuit of one's own needs and drives – in check:

> Hence [...] the ideal's commandment to love one's neighbour as oneself – a commandment which is really justified by the fact that nothing else runs so strongly counter to the original nature of Man.[37]

Despite his many criticisms of civilized society, then, Freud was no revolutionary. Being a doctor and a psychologist, his primary concern was to give courage to the individual, be he healthy or sick, and to enable him to live his life resolutely and with joy.

# Of What Use is Freud's Discovery for Us Today?

## Obeying the Pleasure Principle: Maximizing Pleasure and Avoiding Unpleasure

The appeal which Freud makes to his fellow men is, in the first instance, a clear and simple one. In his psychoanalysis and in his writings he encourages people to lead a self-directed life and to live out, so far as possible, their wishes and desires. Because the whole constitution of Man shows him to be no purely spiritual being independent of Nature, no entity 'made in God's image', but rather, as Freud says, *homo natura*: a natural entity with natural drives and needs. It is, in other words, of the very nature of Man that he strives to entirely satisfy the goals set by his own desires.

The "pleasure principle" – i.e. the striving to maximize pleasure and avoid unpleasure – is an ineradicable part of our animal heritage. Every animal mates when it desires and is able to, eats when it is hungry, and retreats when it senses danger. This "pleasure principle" is also deeply anchored in human nature. Just as feelings of pain warn us against burning ourselves, anxiety and unpleasure warn against whatever might injure the mind. This mechanism has been fulfilling its sensible purpose for millions of years. It both ensures humanity's survival and makes life more pleasant. We avoid encounters, relationships and situations which we experience as threatening, frustrating or tedious and we seek out contacts and situations which we experience as pleasurable, enriching or pleasing. Freud's first, fundamental discovery is as simple as it is self-evident: live in accordance with the "pleasure principle". Wherever possible, maximize pleasure and avoid unpleasure!

## *Id Must Become Ego – From the "Pleasure Principle" to the "Reality Principle"*

But – as Freud, of course, was aware – the fulfilment of our wishes and needs is not always a simple matter and is sometimes quite impossible. Already as a child, and most certainly as an adult, one must accept limitations. In the end, Freud concludes, it is impossible to live unconditionally according to the "pleasure principle":

> This principle (the "pleasure principle") dominates the operation of the mental apparatus from the start. There can be no doubt about its efficacy and yet its programme is at loggerheads with the whole world, with the macrocosm as much as with the microcosm. There is no possibility at all of its being carried through; all the regulations of the universe run counter to it. One feels inclined to say that the intention that man should be 'happy' is not included in the plan of 'Creation'.[38]

It is the tragedy, so to speak, of the faculties which Nature has endowed on Man that he is capable of imagining and wishing for very much more than the real world can ever provide him with. For this reason alone enduring happiness is impossible. Desire may be boundless but reality is not. One cannot always get the thing one desires to eat, live in the place one would like to live, do the job that best realizes one's potentialities, or even be in a relationship of the kind that one ideally envisages for oneself. Life is always a "work in progress". We lack money, or time, or opportunity to comprehensively pursue our wishes; the dream of living purely according to the "pleasure principle" also finds illnesses, accidents, and other small and large catastrophes blocking its way. Even the normal ageing process – one's first grey hairs, one's diminishing bodily vigour – must be accepted as predetermined diminutions of pleasure in life.

Death waits, however, at the end as the greatest of all impositions upon the "pleasure principle". In the last analysis, says Freud, the contradiction between desire for pleasure and reality cannot be reconciled but must be seen as fundamental. That is to say, human existence is itself this contradiction. This is why, for Freud, life's greatest task consists in accepting the conflict between infinite desire and the finitude of reality and making the best of this in a free, upright and honest manner – i.e. free of repressed past experiences, upright in the face of reality's challenges, and honest about one's own needs and also vis-à-vis other human beings. This also involves living with one's defeats, failures and disappointments and not repressing them in a way which will only result in them acquiring power over one's future.

## *Between Scylla and Charybdis – the Secret of Good Upbringing*

But despite the limitations that life imposes on us it is important to articulate one's own needs. A healthy ego, says Freud, accepts its own wishes and desires and tries to work at fulfilling them. But a sense of moderation must be maintained. Some people plan their lives on too grand a scale, cherish too many desires and wishes, and spend their whole lives chasing these wishes' fulfilment. Others, however, make the opposite mistake, are too cautious in their plans and wishes, and end up ruining their lives by asking too little of themselves and the world.

Freud, for his own part, leaned toward the former course; he was highly ambitious and lived constantly in fear of failure. His own mother had early on said to him: "Sigmund, you will surely become someone special". This "prophecy" of his mother's was both a burden on Freud and a spur to ever greater efforts. In his case this combination led to success. But children do not always succeed in living up to the high expectations of their parents and, in their case, the fear of failure becomes a morbid anxiety. Whoever undertakes to bring up children, then, is treading a razor's edge: on the one hand, adults need to spur children on to ever new deeds and achievements; on the other hand, they must get across to them the message that life also involves "doing without". Somewhere in the middle here lies the right way:

> Thus education has to find its way between the Scylla of non-interference and the Charybdis of frustration.[39]

> The child must learn to control his instincts. It is impossible to give him liberty to carry out all his instincts without restriction.
> To do so would be a very instructive experiment for child psychologists;

## Of What Use is Freud's Discovery for Us Today?

> but life would be impossible for the parents and the children themselves would suffer grave damage, which would show itself partly at once and partly in later years. Accordingly, education must inhibit, forbid and suppress, and this it has abundantly seen to in all periods of history.[40]

Upbringing that lacks authority, says Freud, only puts off the day when the child must finally confront that reality which will refuse him many of his wishes and delays his learning of the "reality principle". An overly restrictive upbringing, on the other hand, tends to deprive the child of the courage he will need in order to energetically pursue his ideas and his desires. Freud, therefore, has left us a dual heritage in matters of child-rearing: we must confirm children's desire to act upon the world while at the same time carefully introducing and accustoming them to the minor and major prohibitions of our culture. Because no one can remain a child, and simply follow the prompting of his drives and instincts, all his life. Where id was, there ego must come to be.

## *Anxiety is a Part of Life – Learning to Live Means Learning to Deal with Fear*

What matters, in the end, for the individual is being able to handle his own life. This is not, of course, an easy task. There are days and phases of life when it seems impossible. If the ego finds it has to forgo too many of its wishes, if reality appears insurmountable, or if our own super-ego puts us under too much pressure, then the ego breaks down. It can no longer fulfil its proper function and handle day-to-day life. It succumbs to anxiety in the face of the needs arising from its own drives, being able neither to live these needs out nor to repress them; or to anxiety in the face of reality because it proves no longer to be a match for the demands of the external world; or to anxiety in the form of intense bad conscience vis-à-vis the punitive super-ego, its own idealized image of itself to which it can no longer live up:

> If the ego is obliged to admit its weakness, it breaks out in anxiety – realistic anxiety regarding the external world, moral anxiety regarding the super-ego, and neurotic anxiety regarding the strength of the passions in the id.[41]

This fear of no longer being able to form or direct one's life needs to be averted. The ego thus flees into either neurosis or psychosis. In neurosis the reality that has become unbearable is still acknowledged but sickness becomes a way of avoiding having to deal with it. In psychosis this unbearable reality is simply denied, and replaced by an invented fantasy world.

The mentally healthy individual too reacts with such defence mechanisms. Who has not, at some time or other, caught himself reinterpreting reality in a way less painful for himself and portraying, in his mind, an unpleasant situation in more pleasant terms? Who has not unconsciously avoided an appointment or a meeting by falling sick or by allowing it to "slip his mind"? Whether we do so consciously or unconsciously, and whether we count as mentally unstable or as mentally sound – everyone, says Freud, needs, in the course of handling the task of living, to master conflicts and contradictions. No human life consists of happiness and success alone. And even those of us who are happy are not free of care because they worry about whether their happiness will last.

Basically, then, there is no one who has not known the anxiety of fearing that they might not be able to handle their own life. This fundamental feeling – which seizes us sometimes very strongly, sometimes less so – is, Freud believes, an expression of Man's existential constitution. Because the possibility of feeling afraid springs, in the last analysis, from the fact that human life is not something that just "lives itself". Freud's most profound and perhaps most important message, then, is: anxiety is a part of life.

Where the ego proves unable to handle its proper tasks by drawing on its own forces, and becomes paralyzed by anxiety in the face of existence, Freud speaks of "ego-weakness". The ego, in such a case, needs a break in order to recover its strength. Often, a change as regards work or personal relationships can be enough here. But sometimes the professional help of a doctor or psychologist is also needed. In most cases, however, it suffices that good friends lend an ear to the affected individual and stand by him. This is, after all, what it means to be a human being.

In the debate about whether prior training as a physician was required to practice psychoanalysis Freud himself was a strong advocate of "lay analysis" – i.e. the view that non-medically-qualified people can also offer effective help for mental problems. Such "lay analysis", argued Freud, had been an important form of life-counselling practiced, in various forms, in cultures throughout history. Because the essential basis for the psychoanalytic "talking cure" – namely, tolerance for and openness to the things that are concerning or troubling the other party to the therapeutic talk and the willingness to reflect and interpret this other party's feelings in a free, unforced atmosphere – requires no formal study of medicine. This stance brought down the harsh criticism of the American Psychoanalytical Association on the psychoanalytic profession's own founder, since this powerful organization took the position that only qualified physicians should be allowed to practice psychoanalysis. But Freud stuck to his view that any empathetic and attentive individual is capable of helping others deal with their mental problems. Since all human beings, given what Nature has endowed us with, share similar joys and fears, we are also all, in principle, in a position to understand and interpret the feelings of others.

And this is perhaps the most important part of the legacy Sigmund Freud has left us. He was the first thinker to recognize the profound effects that can be produced by a conversation between one human being and another. Therefore he asked us to weigh our words carefully:

(The word) is the means by which we convey our feelings to one another, our method of influencing other people. Words can do unspeakable good and cause terrible wounds.[42]

# *Bibliographical References:*

1. Civilization and Its Discontents, in The Standard Edition of the Complete Psychological Works of Sigmund Freud, edited by James Strachey and Anna Freud (Hogarth Press and the Institute of Psychoanalysis, London, 1961) (hereinafter abbreviated to Standard Edition), Volume 21, p. 76.
2. A Difficulty in Psychoanalysis, in Standard Edition, Volume 17, p. 141.
3. Ibid. p. 143 (translation slightly revised).
4. The Ego and the Id, in Standard Edition, Volume 19, p.13 (translation slightly revised).
5. The Handling of Dream-Interpretation in Psychoanalysis, in Standard Edition, Volume 12, p. 94.
6. Sigmund Freud to Wilhelm Fliess, in Complete Letters of Sigmund Freud to Wilhelm Fliess, 1887-1904, edited by Jeffrey Masson (University of Chicago Press, 1986) (letter of February 1, 1900) p. 398
7. 'Civilized' Sexual Morality and Modern Nervous Illness, in Standard Edition, Volume 9, p. 191.
8. Three Essays on Sexuality, in Standard Edition, Volume 7, pps. 181-82.
9. Ibid. p. 182.
10. Ibid. p. 207.
11. Introductory Lectures on Psychoanalysis, Part Two, in Standard Edition, Volume 15, p. 207.
12. Ibid.
13. Introductory Lectures on Psychoanalysis, Part Three, in Standard Edition, Volume 16, p. 349.
14. Ibid. p. 414.
15. New Introductory Lectures on Psychoanalysis, in Standard Edition, Volume 22, p. 73.
16. Ibid. p. 77.
17. Ibid. p. 78.
18. The Ego and the Id, in Standard Edition, Volume 19, p. 25.
19. Group Psychology and the Analysis of the Ego, in Standard Edition, Volume 18, p. 90.
20. Ibid.

21 Civilized' Sexual Morality and Modern Nervous Illness, in Standard Edition, Volume 9, p. 187.
22 Ibid.
23 Ibid. p. 191.
24 The Loss of Reality in Neurosis and Psychosis, in Standard Edition, Volume 19, p. 185
25 Ibid.
26 An Outline of Psychoanalysis (1940), in Standard Edition, Volume 23, p. 173.
27 Studies on Hysteria – Psychotherapy of Hysteria, in Standard Edition, Volume 2, p. 305.
28 Advances in Psychoanalytic Therapy in Standard Edition, Volume 17, p. 161.
29 New Introductory Lectures on Psychoanalysis, in Standard Edition, Volume 22, p. 80.
30 The Future of an Illusion in Standard Edition, Volume 21, p. 31.
31 Ibid. p. 49
32 Preface to Theodor Reik's 'Ritual: Psychoanalytic Studies', in Standard Edition, Volume 17, p. 261.
33 The Future of an Illusion in Standard Edition, Volume 21, p. 50.
34 Ibid. p. 12
35 Ibid.
36 Civilization and Its Discontents, in Standard Edition, Volume 21, p. 112.
37 Ibid.
38 Civilization and Its Discontents, in Standard Edition, Volume 21, p. 76.
39 New Introductory Lectures on Psychoanalysis, in Standard Edition, Volume 22, p. 149
40 Ibid.
41 Ibid. p. 78
42 The Question of Lay Analysis in Standard Edition, Volume 20, pps. 187-88.

# *Already published in the same series:*

Walther Ziegler
**Camus in 60 Minutes**
ISBN 9783741227738

Walther Ziegler
**Freud in 60 Minutes**
ISBN 9783741227707

Walther Ziegler
**Hegel in 60 Minutes**
ISBN 9783741227677

Walther Ziegler
**Heidegger in 60 Minutes**
ISBN 9783741227752

Walther Ziegler
**Kant in 60 Minutes**
ISBN 9783741226373

Walther Ziegler
**Marx in 60 Minutes**
ISBN 9783741227691

Walther Ziegler
**Platon in 60 Minutes**
ISBN 9783741227615

Walther Ziegler
**Rousseau in 60 Minutes**
ISBN 9783741227622

Walther Ziegler
**Sartre in 60 Minutes**
ISBN 9783741227653

Walther Ziegler
**Smith in 60 Minutes**
ISBN 9783741227721

## *Coming soon in the same series:*

Walther Ziegler
**Adorno in 60 Minutes**

Walther Ziegler
**Arendt in 60 Minutes**

Walther Ziegler
**Bacon in 60 Minutes**

Walther Ziegler
**Descartes in 60 Minutes**

Walther Ziegler
**Foucault in 60 Minutes**

Walther Ziegler
**Habermas in 60 Minutes**

Walther Ziegler
**Hobbes in 60 Minutes**

Walther Ziegler
**Nietzsche in 60 Minutes**

Walther Ziegler
**Popper in 60 Minutes**

Walther Ziegler
**Rawls in 60 Minutes**

Walther Ziegler
**Schopenhauer in 60 Minutes**

Walther Ziegler
**Wittgenstein in 60 Minutes**

# The author:

Dr Walther Ziegler is academically trained in the fields of philosophy, history and political science. As a foreign correspondent, reporter and newsroom coordinator for the German TV station ProSieben he has produced films on every continent. His news reports have won several prizes and awards. He has also authored numerous books in the field of philosophy. His many years of experience as a journalist mean that he is able to present the complex ideas of the great philosophers in a way that is both engaging and very clear. Since 2007 he has also been active as a teacher and trainer of young TV journalists in Munich, holding the post of Academic Director at the Media Academy, an institute of higher education that offers film and TV courses at its base directly on the site of the major European film production company Bavaria Film.